SCIENTIFIC BOXING

THE DELUXE EDITION

TOGETHER WITH HINTS ON TRAINING AND THE OFFICIAL RULES

James J. Corbett

Heavyweight Champion of the World

PROMETHEAN PRESS

SCIENTIFIC BOXING: THE DELUXE EDITION

Promethean Press
1846 Rosemeade Pkwy #192
Carrollton, TX 75007
www.promethean-press.com

The photograph of Corbett on the cover is by Elmer Chickering, Boston.

"A Recollection of the Fight Between John L. Sullivan and James J. Corbett" taken from the book *Inside Facts on Pugilism* by George Siler. Laird and Lee. 1907.

Manufactured in the United States of America

ISBN 978-0-9737698-9-0

TABLE OF CONTENTS

PART TWO: FOULS

PART THREE: RULES FOR BOXING

ADDENDUM

PREFACE

There is no man in the world who is better qualified to write a boxing book for young men and boys than James J. Corbett. His style, speed and cleverness were a revelation to those followers of that old school where to take a blow in order to give one was considered the proper thing.

He was the ideal American boxer, scientific, elusive and accurate, mapping out a plan of battle with the care and foresight of an army general on the eve of an important engagement.

From the first he raised the sport to a higher

James Jeffries and James Corbett - June 30, 1910, Moana Springs, Nevada

plane and convinced the public that a man who fought championship battles was not necessarily uncouth, untaught nor unlettered.

His sobriquet of "Gentleman Jim" is an uncommon and unusual one, but those who know him personally understand how well he deserves it.

Jas J Jeffries

JAMES J. JEFFRIES
Ex-Champion of the World

INTRODUCTION
BOXING AS A SCIENCE

If every young man in America would take up boxing as a pastime we would have better men and better citizens. In my many years' experience in athletics I have come to the conclusion that there is more actual benefit to be derived from it than from any other form of exercise.

It develops every muscle in the human body, it quickens the brain, it sharpens the wits, it imparts force, and above all it teaches self-control.

If some clever scientist were to discover an herb, or concoct a medicine with which he could guarantee to accomplish half of that, there is no factory in the world which would be big enough to manufacture sufficient to supply the demand.

In this "hurry up" age men think too little of their health and their physical welfare to bother about putting on a pair of gloves, and so this book is not for them. It is for the boys and young men. It is for Young America that I have written.

I was just the same kind of a boy as any other boy is, fond of life and outdoor sport, but not too rugged. If it had not been for boxing I might be the most ordinary man today. I took up boxing simply as an exercise and instead of thinking it meant nothing more than putting on a pair of padded gloves and slamming wildly away at another fellow's head, I figured

Fitzsimmons landing his solar plexus blow on Jeffries.

out that there was a lot to be learned about hitting, blocking and getting away.

So I made a study of it, and that study resulted in my gaining the title of heavyweight champion of the world, by beating a man who had held the title for twelve years.

Boxing is a good healthy exercise for anyone, and when I say boxing I don't mean slugging. Don't try to be a hard hitter before you know what you are going to hit and how you are going to hit.

Think; use your brains; they figure in boxing just as much as do the gloves. Look your opponent squarely in the eye and try to discover his weak point. Find out if you can his line of attack, and then try to defeat it.

The average amateur boxes with the same set series of movements. He leads high, then he leads low, then he swings, and so on through a routine, as if he was a mechanical toy, wound up to go through a certain set series of movements, and then stop.

Whatever else you do, think, be versatile and clever. You don't need to be a ruffian or a loafer to be a boxer, and boxing doesn't lower a young man. It makes him better. If I were asked to advise the boys of the United States, in a few words I would say: "Put on the gloves."

The good boxer must lead a regular life, and that means good hours. Dissipation has ruined more great athletes than all other causes combined. So if you want to be a good boxer, you must be in good physical health. And if you want health, strength and

A left lead or a jab should be landed this way.

speed, you will have to train for it.

By training I don't mean to go through the regular and severe course that is preparatory and preliminary to a great contest, but I mean the sensible training that is within the capabilities of every young man, whether he is working for a living or not.

Assume, for the sake of argument, that a young fellow is employed during the day. Arising a half-hour earlier in the morning would be no great hardship if he wanted to do so. The time so gained could be spent in road work one morning, and indoor exercise the next, It might, if his hours of business were long, come a little hard at first, but he would soon get used to it, and by that time he would so have improved his physical condition that it could stand many times the extra tax put upon it.

Bear in mind that thirty minutes a day will work wonders in three months, and in even shorter time than that if the work is mapped out properly and done conscientiously.

Don't cultivate big muscles; leave those to the weightlifters. The ideal boxer wants strength and muscle, but he doesn't want to be muscle bound; that is something I have always steered clear of.

Keep away from big weights. Dumbbells should not be heavier than two pounds each. Work with something that cultivates speed, and the necessary strength will come with it.

Footwork is a most important part of modern boxing, and by modern I mean what the title of this book implies.

Footwork may be practiced without an opponent - just imagine you are boxing and put up your hands. Feint, step in, then back, then first to one side, then to the other, but work fast, all the while keeping up your feinting and your balance on your toes. No matter in what position you may be, bear in mind it must always be one in which you are prepared to attack,

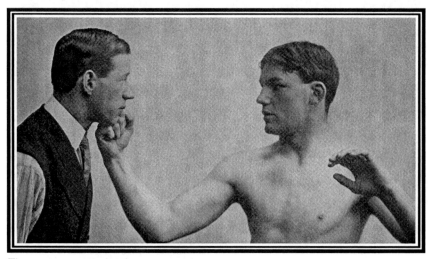

The proper way to land an uppercut.

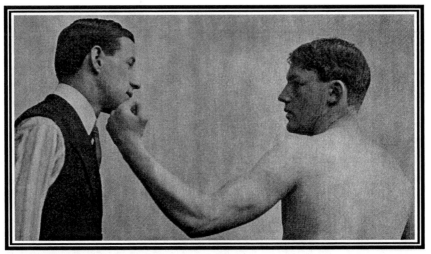

A left hook should be delivered in this manner.

defend or retreat, So really it resolves itself into a question of headwork, and that is what you must cultivate most.

But whether training, or working, or at play, bear in mind one thing, and it is that fresh air is absolutely necessary to health. I have advised road work, not only because it will strengthen the body, but also because it will supply the lungs with fresh air. Breathe deeply - when you breathe pure, fresh air - and you will breathe properly. Feed your lungs as you would feed your stomach; they need it as much and even more, but don't cool off in fresh air after you have exercised and when you are overheated, unless you are well wrapped up.

This brings me naturally to the subject of baths. The act of plunging suddenly into cold water is apt to produce a shock which is not good, so don't think simply because you have read about it somewhere that a cold plunge is essential, for it is not. A gradual

Showing the position of the fist for a straight right.

cooling off and a good rubdown will answer the purpose, and when you want a bath, take the chill off the water. Warm water soothes and refreshes, and after some great effort in which the strength has been taxed nothing will restore nature so quickly as a warm bath. What I do consider good for any young man is a cold sponge in the morning, but that is quite different from the plunge.

If you are going to train you will have to stop smoking, for it is rank poison to the athlete. Inveterate smokers don't make champions in any class or any branch of athletics. If you smoke a great deal, cut it down one-half and you will notice within a short time a marked improvement in your condition.

Summed up in a few words I should say to the young amateur: don't drink intoxicating liquors, don't smoke, exercise regularly, breath plenty of fresh air, and keep your temper when boxing.

In these few lines are condensed what might make an entire book, but any story is well told if told simply, and, besides simplicity and brevity, it is more apt to make an impression which will be retained.

On the question of diet, many men have many ideas, but I consider regular meals the first step. Then study your own stomach and eat what agrees with you, but not to excess. It would be an absurd proposition for me to attempt to dictate to a class of one hundred young men what they should and what they should not eat, because what agrees with one might not agree with another.

In the old days of the London prize ring there were hard and fast rules for training. Today they are to be laughed at. They may have been all right for those men and those days, but they would not do now. They did not look for speed then, but rather developed a physique that was oak - like in its strength, and cultivated a blow that would fell an ox - if it landed. Blows like that are too easily avoided nowadays, and the man who feints and sidesteps has to be reckoned with.

PART ONE
FUNDAMENTALS

HOW TO STAND

Usually the first question the amateur boxer asks is: "How shall I stand?"

While he may be taught how to hold his hands in a manner which will best suit the purposes of offense and defense, yet the position he will eventually settle into is one which will come natural to him.

Plate No. 1, opposite, posed for by Billy Britt, once the amateur champion lightweight, is businesslike as well as simple. It is well set, with the right ready for instant and effective action, but it is not really of the modern school, in which footwork plays a most important part. It is the position of a man who is there to hold his ground and swap punches.

A GOOD POSITION

Here is the pose of the alert, resourceful boxer, both of whose hands are in readiness to deliver a blow at an instant's notice. It is well balanced and well protected. The stomach is partly covered, and the raising of the left shoulder will guard the jaw. It shows Jimmy Britt at his best. The left is in a position to do its most effective long-range work, because it is in the best possible position for reach.

READY FOR INFIGHTING

Without changing the position of the feet, which are well braced for the body to receive the shock of an attack, the position shown on the opposite page can be assumed, and the boxer is prepared to cover up, counter, side-step or break ground. He can feint rapidly, so as to confuse an opponent. He can also step in so as to draw a lead.

THE CROUCH

Here it is assumed he is meeting the onward rush of an opponent. He blocks the first blow or two and then makes that attack with both hands on the stomach, for which Jimmy Britt, Terry McGovern and Frankie Neil are famous, and which has invariably proven terribly effective, even against the most clever opponents.

BLOCKING

Never block with the closed hand, as the open hand furnishes as much protection again as the clenched fist, and the proportion is even greater when the gloves are on. The illustration on the opposite page shows how to block a lead or a swing for the jaw, and the left hand is drawn back ready for a counter or a drive to the stomach.

DUCKING

There are many cases where it is advisable to duck a lead for the head, and it is illustrated here. It also shows the boxer, while the blow intended for him has gone harmlessly over his head, reaching his opponent's stomach with a straight left, except that in this instance the knuckles of his hand are thrown too far back. The result of a blow of this kind, if properly delivered, cannot be underestimated.

A SHORT ARM PUNCH

You will notice that the position of the feet in all of these illustrations is practically the same, and the man who stands right can attack and defend at will. Personally I believe in foot work - the more rapid, the better. On the opposite page the boxer is shown lunging forward to deliver a right jab. The action of but one arm is shown, as it is intended to demonstrate that particular move. The left should be held well forward, with the palm out, so as to block the more readily. But the young boxer will soon have a style of his own after he has become familiar with the gloves.

AT THE CALL OF TIME

The preliminary to all bouts is the handshake, and should never be omitted. Bear in mind that you are not going to engage in a mortal combat. Boxing should train the mind as it develops the body, and the young man who loses his head or temper should indulge in some other branch of sport. A clear, quick brain is as necessary in a boxing contest as gloves are.

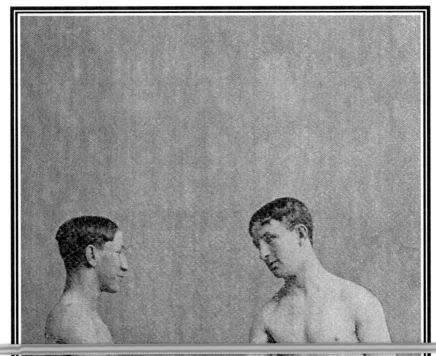

ON GUARD

And now on guard. Don't think you have got to land the first punch, although it is policy to do so, if you can, without leaving yourself open for a damaging counter. Study your opponent carefully; note the position of his feet and how he holds his hands. Study out and discover, if you can, his weak points and plan out your mode of attack. If he guards high, lead low, and vice versa, as he will usually guard his most tender spot. A clever boxer can cause a man to shift his guard at will.

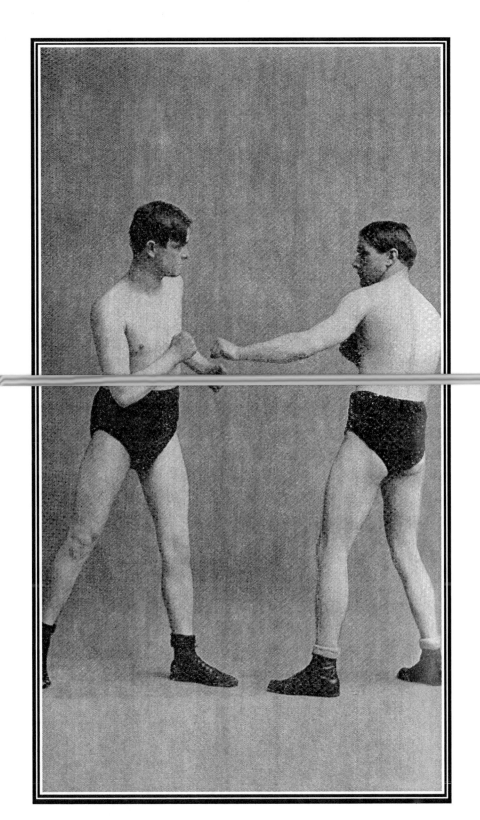

THE LEFT LEAD

This shows the first punch usually taught by all instructors - the left lead, but it doesn't show the guard for a counter, for the reason that a fast two-handed boxer is usually inclined to take chances, and instead of using his free hand for a block, punches with it as soon as his lead lands. In these days of scientific boxing it is usually the fast, scientific man who wins out, so from the first the amateur is encouraged to develop speed and precision.

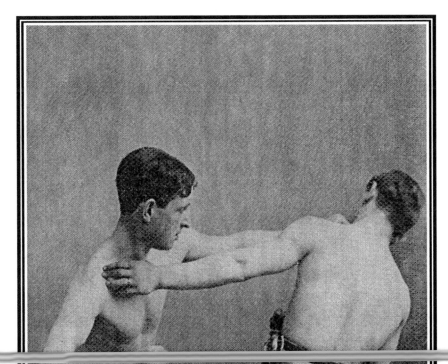

ONE WAY TO BLOCK

This is one way to block (or throw off) a left lead. The incoming arm is caught at the wrist - not held - and thrown violently upward. Step in quickly, at the same time driving the right to the stomach. If the body and the arm work together in harmony the power of the blow will be immeasurably increased.

CROSSING ON THE JAW

This left lead has been sidestepped just enough to allow the hand to go over the shoulder. It can, when necessary, be thrown off in the same manner with the open hand, but sidestepping a punch has the advantage of leaving both hands free for attack. The right is then crossed - as shown - to the jaw, but it must he done quickly and accurately to be effective.

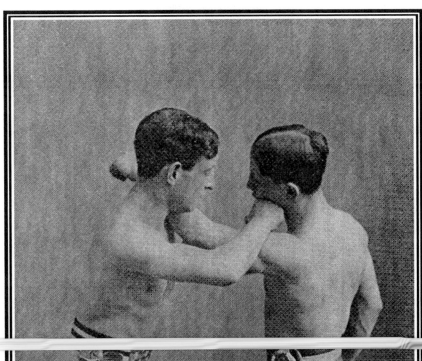

DUCKING A LEAD

The art of ducking to guard a blow is one that must be thoroughly practiced. Avoiding a lead by ducking is one thing and running into an uppercut is another, and it takes a good man to get away with it. In the illustration opposite the boxer (Jimmy Britt), who has assumed a crouching position, has taken advantage of his move to land a right to the body. It would be just as well to figure this out in advance and try it at the first left lead. But look out for the uppercut.

LEFT LEAD WITH GUARD

Here is a left-hand punch well delivered at close quarters, with the left shoulder preventing a possible counter on the jaw. The right is ready to stop a return, or it can be hooked sharply to the body. Young boxers cannot pay too much attention to the development of the left hand, as it is always half way there, and frequent jabs with it are bound to discon-cert the most aggressive and coolest opponent.

LEFT HOOK TO THE BODY

Technically this is known as infighting, and is usually disastrous to an opponent, particularly when both hands are used. As mentioned before, the safest way is to step inside a lead. The body should work with the arms, so as to give more force to the blows. A punch with the force of the body behind it, and driving it home, is much more punishing, naturally, than it would be if only the arm supplied the power.

LANDING ON THE SOLAR PLEXUS

The solar plexus is that part of the body which is situated directly below the front chest cavity, and is a nerve center. A blow which lands fairly, while it does not produce a knockout, usually paralyzes the recipient and renders him incapable of further effort for the time being. It is usually delivered in the form of a half arm punched with the full weight of the body behind it.

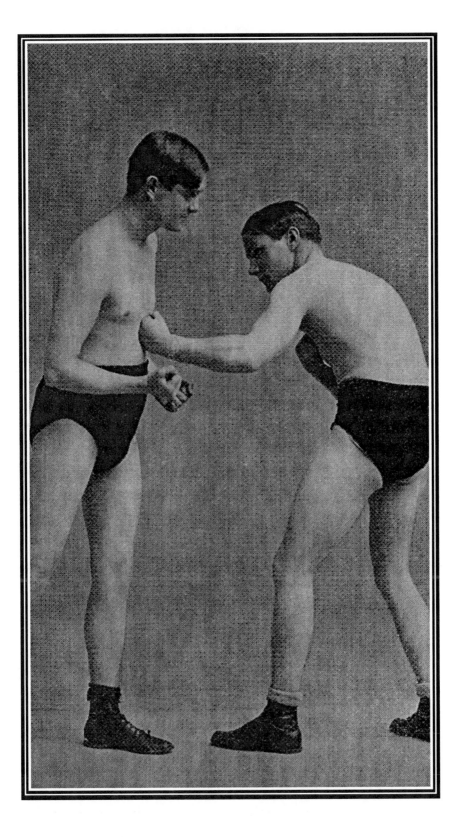

SIDESTEPPING

A good way to avoid a blow is to sidestep, which, as the word implies, means to step from in front of an opponent making a lead to one side of him, To be effective and successful it must be done smartly and decisively, without any suggestion of feinting, which will defeat its ultimate object. In sidestepping a punch intended for the head, the cool boxer will usually find an opening for the body, where a swinging or half arm left can very readily be placed.

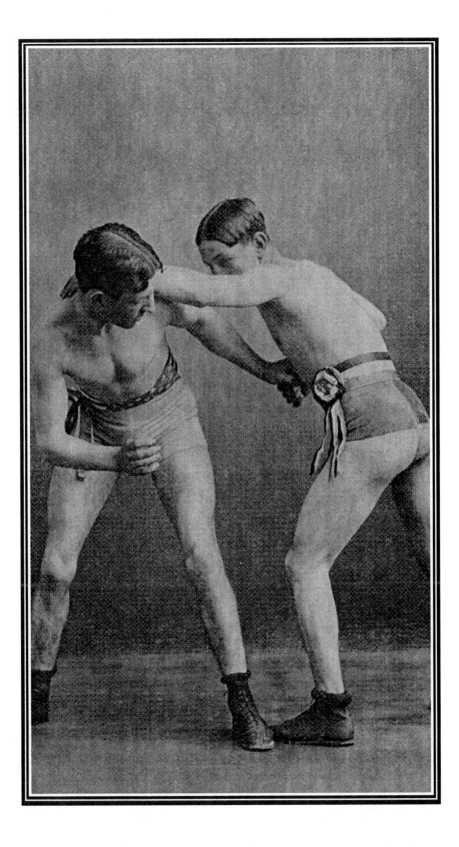

HOOK BLOWS

A hook is, as its name implies, a short, sharp jolt delivered with either hand, and it is only used at close quarters. The illustration opposite shows a right hook to the jaw, which was made possible by stepping inside a left lead. To be effective the full force of the upper part of the body should be behind a hook. Being a short arm blow it does not call for the same amount of accuracy or judgment of distance as a swing or a straight lead, but it can be perfected with practice.

INFIGHTING

On the opposite page Frankie Neil demonstrates that series of blows which has come to be known as infighting, in which both hands are used against the body of an opponent, usually with telling effect. The best way in which to deliver these blows is to work close in and set a fast pace. Wait for a lead and step inside of it, and then stay there. But never attempt it unless you are inside the other fellow's guard.

BLOCKING A SWING

When you see your opponent is about to swing there are several things to do, but they must be done quickly. In the first place it can be stopped just after it starts, as shown on the opposite page; it can be blocked by the glove just before it lands; it can be ducked, or you can step in and let it go around your neck. In the latter case, you can usually land a stiff body punch as you step in. If it is stopped before it is well under way - and only a quick boxer can do that - it usually throws the man who starts it off his balance, and a speedy boxer can smother him with blows before he has a chance to set himself.

THE UPPER CUT

The upper cut is always delivered at short range, and is a short, sharp, snappy punch, which lands on the point of the jaw unless your opponent is ducking at the time when it lands full on the face. When well delivered, and with force behind it, it is a most damaging blow. Many young boxers have a habit of rushing in head downward. In cases of this kind a well-directed upper cut will usually straighten them up.

THE KIDNEY PUNCH

The kidneys are a particularly vulnerable spot and repeated blows over them are bound to take the steam out of a man. There are several ways of landing it, but the simplest is during a clinch. They can also be reached by sidestepping a left, throwing the arm up, as shown in the accompanying illustration when a speedy man can usually land two or more blows.

SIDESTEPPING

Too much cannot be said of the value of side-stepping, and it is here exemplified again. But simple sidestepping to avoid punishment is like a job half done. The man who uses his head as well as his hands and feet will usually figure it out so as to deliver a blow at the same time he avoids one. That is shown in this instance, where a short arm jolt reaches the stomach.

THE KNOCKOUT BLOW

What is known as the knockout punch is landed on the jaw usually on the side. It can be delivered from the side or in front. The force of the blow necessary to produce unconsciousness depends upon two things - the jaw that is hit and the power of the blow. A comparatively light punch will be sufficient for the average untrained man, while there are some professional boxers whom it is almost impossible to knock out, because of the strength and formation of their jaws. If you are boxing for amusement and exercise, don't try the knockout.

PART TWO
FOULS

HOLDING

When you do box, box clean. Don't hold or take an unfair advantage. The placing of your hand around your opponent's neck, as shown on the opposite page, constitutes holding, and is a foul. When you get in a clinch, break clean. Read the rules and abide by them, and bear in mind that boxing is not fighting. Learn the science of the game. The inflicting of needless punishment upon an inferior opponent doesn't add anything to your laurels, and it tends to lower the high status of the game.

USING THE ELBOW

This is a very unfair blow, and when it is done it is done deliberately. The foul is a most flagrant one. The right is led so it will go past your opponent's head, and in bringing the arm back; the elbow is used against the jaw.

HITTING WHEN DOWN

To hit a man when he is down means to strike him when any part of his body except his feet touches the floor. A man on one knee is down. When your opponent is down, step back and give him a chance to get up. Don't lose your head and rush at him wildly. Be calm and take your time.

MISUSE OF THE GLOVE

The blow which is shown here is foul, because the heel of the glove is used, but it is not always a deliberate one, as many young boxers, in the excitement of a bout, will do things which they know are wrong. So in striking a blow be careful to strike with the fist clenched, as that is the way it is intended it should be used.

BUTTING

It quite frequently happens that during a bout one boxer's head will come in contact with the head of an opponent, and in many cases the foul was intended. There is an inclination, however, on the part of many boxers to butt, which ought to be discouraged. The man with a cool head never makes any mistakes like that, and the fellow who uses his head would do anything that was unfair.

ANOTHER FOUL

Don't put the palm of your glove over an opponent's nose to stop his breathing, or don't use it to push his head back, as shown by the accompanying illustration, for both are foul. Remember that boxing gloves are made to punch with.

PART THREE
RULES OF BOXING

MARQUIS OF QUEENSBERRY RULES

RULE 1

To be a fair stand-up boxing match in a 24-foot ring, or as near that size as practicable.

RULE 2

No wrestling or hugging allowed.

RULE 3

The rounds are to be of three minutes' duration, and one-minute time between rounds.

RULE 4

If either man fall, through weakness or otherwise, he must get up unassisted, ten seconds to be allowed him to do so, the other man meanwhile to return to his corner, and when the fallen man is on his legs the round is to be resumed and continued until the three minutes have expired. If one man fails to come to the scratch in the ten seconds allowed, it shall be in the power of the referee to give his award in favor of the other man.

RULE 5

A man hanging on the ropes in a helpless state, with his toes off the ground, shall be considered down.

Jack Broughton (1734-1750), *father of
first boxing rules.*

RULE 6
No seconds or any other person to be allowed in the ring during the rounds.

RULE 7
Should the contest be stopped by any unavoidable interference, the referee to name time and place, as soon as possible, for finishing the contest; so that the match must be won and lost, unless the backers of both men agree to draw the stakes.

RULE 8
The gloves are to be fair-sized boxing gloves of the best quality, and new.

RULE 9
Should a glove burst or come off, it must be replaced to the referee's satisfaction.

RULE 10
A man on one knee is considered down and if struck is entitled to the stakes.

RULE 11
No shoes or boots with springs allowed.

RULE 12
The contest in all other respects to be governed by revised rules of the London Prize Ring.

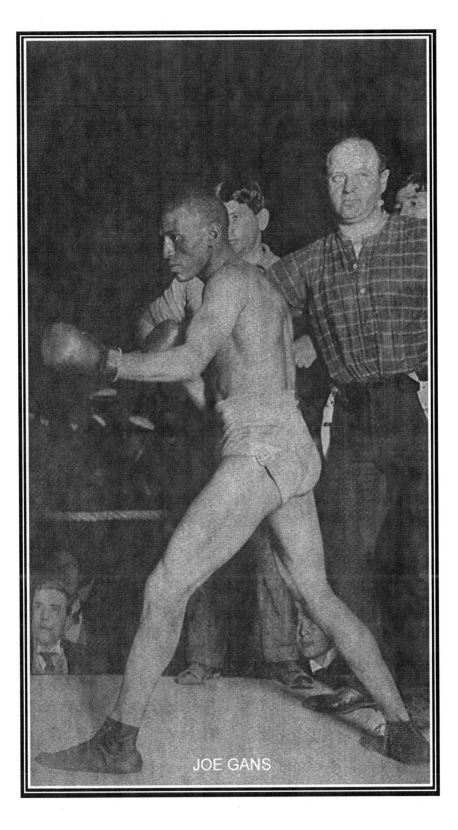

JOE GANS

"POLICE GAZETTE"
REVISED QUEENSBERRY RULES

RULE 1
The weights for all pugilists who contend in glove contests, according to the "Police Gazette" boxing rules, shall be as follows: for heavyweights, over 158 lbs.; middle, under 158 lbs. and over 140 lbs.; light, under 140 lbs.

RULE 2
All contests are to be decided in a 24-foot ring, which must be erected on the ground or stage.

RULE 3
No wrestling or hugging allowed. The rounds are to be of three minutes' duration and one-minute time.

RULE 4
Each contestant shall select an umpire, and they shall appoint a referee.

RULE 5
In all contests two timekeepers shall be appointed, and the referee, under no circumstances, shall keep time.

PHILADELPHIA JACK O'BRIEN

RULE 6

During the contest, if either man fall, through weakness or otherwise, he must get up unassisted, ten seconds being allowed him to do so, the other man meanwhile to retire to his corner, and when the fallen man is on his legs the round is to be resumed and continued until the three minutes have expired; and if one man fails to come to the scratch in the ten seconds allowed, it shall rein the power of the referee to give his award in favor of the other man.

RULE 7

A contestant hanging on the ropes in a helpless state, with his toes off the ground, shall be considered down. No seconds, or any other person but the referee to be allowed in the ring.

RULE 8

Should the contest be stopped by any unavoidable interference, the referee, if appointed, or else the stakeholder, shall name the next time and place for finishing the contest, as soon as possible, so that the match must be either won or lost.

RULE 9

When either pugilist is knocked down within the allotted three minutes, he shall be allowed ten seconds to get on his feet again unassisted, except when this occurs in the last ten seconds.

AURELIA "THE MEXICAN" HERRERA

RULE 10

One minute's rest shall be allowed between each round; and no wrestling, roughing or struggling on the ropes shall be permitted.

RULE 11

The gloves are to be fair-sized boxing gloves, of the best quality and new. Should a glove burst or come off, it must be replaced to the referee's satisfaction. A man on one knee is considered down, and if struck, is entitled to the stakes. No shoes or boots with spikes allowed.

RULE 12

In all matches the stakes not to be given up until won or lost by a fight. That if a man leaves the ring, either to escape punishment or for any other purpose, without the permission of the referee, unless he is involuntarily forced out, shall forfeit the battle.

RULE 13

That any pugilist voluntarily quitting the ring, previous to the deliberate judgment of the referee being obtained, shall be deemed to have lost the fight.

RULE 14

That the seconds shall not interfere, advise or direct the adversary of their principal, and shall refrain from all offensive and irritating expressions, in all respects conducting themselves with order and

JOHN L. SULLIVAN

decorum, and consign themselves to the diligent and careful discharge of their duties to their principals.

RULE 15

If either man shall willfully throw himself down without receiving a blow, whether blows shall have been previously exchanged or not, he shall be deemed to have lost the battle; but that this rule shall not apply to a man who, in a close, slips down from the grasp of an opponent to avoid punishment or from obvious accident or weakness. The battle-money shall remain in the hands of the stakeholder until fairly won or lost by a fight, unless a draw be mutually agreed upon, or in case of a postponement one of the principals shall be absent, when the man in the ring shall be awarded the stakes.

RULE 16

In contests in which contestants agree to box four, six or a stipulated number of rounds, the referee shall have full power to order the men to continue, if it has not been decided during the four, six or number of rounds stipulated by one or the other of the pugilists stopping, losing by a foul or being beaten.

OSCAR "BATTLING" NELSON

LONDON PRIZE-RING RULES

RULE 1
That the ring shall be made on turf, and shall be four-and-twenty feet square, formed of eight stakes and ropes, the latter extending in double lines, the uppermost line being four feet from the ground, and the lower two feet from the ground. That in the center of the ring a mark be formed, to be termed a "Scratch."

RULE 2
That each man shall be attended to the ring by two seconds and a bottle-holder. That the combatants, on shaking hands, shall retire until the seconds of each have tossed for choice of position, which adjusted, the winner shall choose his corner according to the state of the wind or sun, and conduct his man thereto; the loser taking the opposite diagonal corner.

RULE 3
That each man shall be provided with a handkerchief of a color suitable to his own fancy, and that the seconds shall entwine these handkerchiefs at the upper end of one of the center stakes. That these handkerchiefs shall be called "Colors," and that the winner of the battle at its conclusion shall be entitled to their possession as the trophy of victory.

YOUNG CORBETT

RULE 4

That two umpires shall be chosen by the seconds or backers to watch the progress of the battle, and take exception to any breach of the rules hereafter stated. That a referee shall be chosen by the umpires, unless otherwise agreed on, to whom all disputes shall be referred; and that the decision of this referee, whatever it may be, shall be final and strictly binding on all parties, whether as to the matter in dispute or the issue of the battle. That this official shall receive out of the stakes a sum of five percent for officiating, such sum to be deducted by the stakeholder either from the amount of the winnings in the case of a win, or in equitable proportions from each stake in the event of a draw. No payment to be made in the event of a forfeit or of the referee not being called upon to act. That the umpires shall be provided with a watch for the purpose of calling time; and that they mutually agree upon which this duty shall devolve, the call of that umpire only to be attended to, and no other person whatever, except the referee when appealed to, shall interfere in calling time. That the referee shall withhold all opinion till appealed to by the umpires, and that the umpires strictly abide by his decision without dispute.

RULE 5

That on the men being stripped, it shall be the duty of the seconds to examine their drawers, and if any objection arises as to insertion of improper sub-

TERRY McGOVERN

stances therein, they shall appeal to their umpires, who, with the concurrence of the referee, shall direct what alterations shall be made.

RULE 6

That the spikes in the lighting boots shall be confined to three in number, which shall not exceed three-eighths of an inch from the sole of the boot, and shall not be less than one-eighth of an inch broad at the point; two to be placed in the broadest part of the sole and one in the heel; and that in the event of a man wearing any other spikes either in the toes or elsewhere, he shall be compelled either to remove them or provide other boots properly spiked, the penalty for refusal to be a loss of the stakes.

RULE 7

That both men being ready, each shall be conducted to that side of the scratch next his corner previously chosen; and the seconds on the one side, and the men on the other, having shaken hands, the former shall immediately leave the ring and there remain till the round be finished, on no pretense whatever approaching their principals during the round, without permission from the referee. The penalty to be the loss of the battle to the offending parties.

KID McCOY

RULE 8.

That at the conclusion of the round, when one or both of the men shall be down, the seconds shall step into the ring and carry or conduct their principal to his corner, there affording him the necessary assistance, and that no person whatever be permitted to interfere in his duty.

RULE 9

That on the expiration of thirty seconds the umpire appointed shall cry "Time," upon which each man shall rise from the knee of his second and walk to his own side of the scratch unaided; the seconds immediately leaving the ring. The penalty for either of them remaining eight seconds after the call of time to be the loss of the battle to his principal; and that either man failing to be at the scratch within eight seconds shall be deemed to have lost the battle.

RULE 10

That on no consideration whatever shall any person, except the seconds or the referee, be permitted to enter the ring during the battle, nor till it shall have been concluded; and that in the event of such unfair practice, or the ropes or stakes being disturbed or removed, it shall be in the power of the referee to award the victory to that man who, in his honest opinion, shall have the best of the contest.

RAY BRONSON

RULE 11

That the seconds shall not interfere, advise, or direct the adversary of their principal, and shall refrain from all offensive and irritating expressions, in all respects conducting themselves with order and decorum, and confine themselves to the diligent and careful discharge of their duties to their principals.

RULE 12

That in picking up their men, should the seconds willfully injure the antagonist of their principal, the latter shall be deemed to have forfeited the battle on the decision of the referee.

RULE 13

That it shall be a fair "stand up fight" and if either man shall willfully throw himself down without receiving a blow, whether blows shall have previously been exchanged or not, he shall be deemed to have lost the battle; but that this rule shall not apply to a man who in a close slips down from the grasp of his opponent to avoid punishment, or from obvious accident or weakness.

RULE 14

That butting with the head shall be deemed foul, and the party resorting to this practice shall be deemed to have lost the battle.

"CLEVER" TOMMY MURPHY

RULE 15

That a blow struck when a man is thrown or down shall be deemed foul. That a man with one knee and one hand on the ground, or with both knees on the ground, shall be deemed down; and a blow given in either of those positions shall be considered foul, providing always that, when in such position, the man so down shall not himself strike or attempt to strike.

RULE 16

That a blow struck below the waistband shall be deemed foul, and that, in a close, seizing an antagonist below the waist, by the thigh or otherwise shall be deemed foul.

RULE 17

That all attempts to inflict injury by gouging, or tearing the flesh with the fingers or nails, and biting, shall be deemed foul.

RULE 18

That kicking or deliberately falling on an antagonist with the knees (or otherwise when down) shall be deemed foul.

RULE 19

That all bets shall be paid as the battle money, after a fight, is awarded.

RUBEN WARNES

RULE 20

The referee and umpires shall take their positions in front of the center stake outside the ropes.

RULE 21

That due notice shall be given by the stakeholder of the day and place where the battle money is to be given up, and that he be exonerated from all responsibility upon obeying the direction of the referee; that all parties be strictly bound by these rules; and that in future all articles of agreement for a contest be entered into with a strict and willing adherence to the letter and spirit of these rules.

RULE 22

That in the event of magisterial or other interference, or in case of darkness coming on, the referee (or stakeholder in case no referee has been chosen) shall have the power to name the time and place for the next meeting, if possible on the same day, or as soon after as may be. In naming the second or third place, the nearest spot shall be selected to the original place of fighting where there is a chance of its being fought out.

RULE 23

That should the light not be decided on the day all bets shall be drawn, unless the fight shall be resumed the same week, between Sunday and Sunday, in which case the referee's duties shall con-

JOHNNY DOUGLAS

tinue, and the bets shall stand and be decided by the event. The battle money shall remain in the hands of the stakeholder until fairly won or lost by a fight, unless a draw be mutually agreed upon, or, in case of a postponement, one of the principals shall be absent, when the man in the ring shall be awarded the stakes.

RULE 24
That any pugilist voluntarily quitting the ring, previous to the deliberate judgment of the referee being obtained, shall be deemed to have lost the fight.

RULE 25
That on an objection being made by the seconds or umpire the men shall retire to their corners, and there remain until the decision of the appointed authorities shall be obtained; that if pronounced "foul," the battle shall be at an end; but if "fair," "time" shall be called by the party appointed, and the man absent from the scratch in eight seconds after shall be deemed to have lost the fight. The decision in all cases to be given promptly and irrevocably, for which purpose the umpires and the referee should be invariably close together.

RULE 26
That if a man leaves the ring, either to escape punishment or for any other purpose, without the permission of the referee, unless he is involuntarily

TOMMY RYAN

forced out, shall forfeit the battle.

RULE 27

That the use of hard substances, such as stones, or sticks or of resin in the hand during the battle, shall be deemed foul, and that on the requisition of the seconds of either man the accused shall open his hands for the examination of the referee.

RULE 28

That hugging on the ropes shall be deemed foul. That a man held by the neck against the stakes, or upon or against the ropes, shall be considered down, and all interference with him in that position shall be foul.

That if a man in any way makes use of the ropes or stakes to aid him in squeezing his adversary, he shall be deemed the loser of the battle; and that if a man in a close reaches the ground with his knees, his adversary shall immediately loose him or lose the battle.

RULE 29

That all glove or room fights be as nearly as possible in conformity with the foregoing rules.

FRED RUSSELL

AMATEUR ATHLETIC UNION RULES

RULE 1
In all open competitions the ring shall not be less than 16 feet or more than 24 feet square, and shall be formed of eight stakes and ropes, the latter extending in double lines, the uppermost line four feet from the floor and the lower line two feet from the floor.

RULE 2
Competitors to box in regulation athletic costume, in shoes without spikes, or in socks, and to use boxing gloves of not more than eight ounces in weight.

RULE 3
Weights to be: Bantam, 105 lbs. and under; Feather, 115 lbs. and under; Light, 135 lbs. and under; Middle, 158 lbs. and under; Heavy Weight, 158 lbs. and over.

RULE 4
Any athlete who weighs in and then fails to compete, without an excuse satisfactory to the Games Committee, shall be suspended for six months.

RULE 5
In all open competitions the result shall be decided by two judges with a referee. A timekeeper shall be appointed.

"UTAH" BOB THOMPSON

RULE 6

In all competitions the number of rounds to be contested shall be three. The duration of rounds in the trial bout shall be limited to three minutes each. In the "finals," the first two rounds will be three minutes each and the final round four minutes. The interval between each round shall be one minute.

RULE 7

In all competitions, any competitor failing to come up when time is called shall lose the bout.

RULE 8

Immediately before the competition, each competitor shall draw his number and compete as follows: to have a preliminary round of as many contests as the total number of contestants exceeds 2, 4, 8, 16, or 32 and drop the losers. This leaves in 2, 4, 8, 16 or 32 contestants, and the rounds then proceed regularly, with no byes or uneven contests.

RULE 9

Each competitor shall be entitled to the assistance of one second only, and no advice or coaching shall be given to any competitor by his second, or by any other person during the progress of any round.

RULE 10

The manner of judging shall be as follows: The two judges and referee shall be stationed apart. At the

JIMMY GARDNER

end of each bout, each judge shall write the name of the competitor who in his opinion has won and shall hand the same to the announcer (or master of ceremonies). In case the judges agree, the master of ceremonies shall announce the name of the winner, but in cases where the judges disagree, the master of ceremonies shall so inform the referee, who shall thereupon himself decide.

RULE 11
The referee shall have power to give his casting vote when the judges disagree to caution or disqualify a competitor for infringing rules, or to stop a round in the event of either man being knocked down, providing that the stopping of either of the first two rounds shall not disqualify any competitor from competing in the final round; to decide the competition in the event of either man showing so marked a superiority over the other that a continuation of the contest would serve only to show the loser's ability to take punishment. And the referee can order a further round, limited to two minutes, in the event of the judges disagreeing.

RULE 12
The decision of the judges or referee, as the case may be, shall be final.

RULE 13
In all competitions the decision shall be given in

MIKE GLOVER

favor of the competitor who displays the best style, and obtains the greatest number of points. The points shall be: for attack, direct clean hits with the knuckles of either hand, on any part of the front or sides of the head, or body above the belt; defense, guarding, slipping, ducking, counter-hitting or getting away. Where points are otherwise equal, consideration to be given the man who does most of the leading off.

RULE 14

The referee may disqualify a competitor who is boxing unfairly, by flicking or hitting with the open glove, by hitting with the inside or butt of the hand, the wrist or elbow, hitting or catching hold below the waist, or hitting when down (one knee and one hand or both knees on the floor), butting with the head or shoulder, wrestling or roughing at the ropes, using offensive and scurrilous language, or not obeying the orders of the referee.

RULE 15

All competitors who have been beaten by the winner shall be entitled to compete for second place, and all who have been beaten by the winners of either first or second place shall be entitled to compete for third place.

RULE 16

Any athlete who competes in a boxing contest of

JIMMY CLABBY

more than four rounds shall be suspended for such, the stated period as may be determined by the Board of Managers of the association of the Amateur Athletic Union, in whose territory the offense was committed.

RULE 17

In the event of any question arising not provided for in these rules, the referee to have full power to decide such question or interpretation of rule.

JACK JOHNSON

ADDENDUM

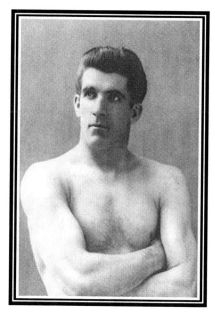

A Recollection of the Fight Between
John L. Sullivan and James J. Corbett

After Sullivan defeated Kilrain in the last championship battle under London prize ring rules, it was thought he would retire on his well-earned laurels. He was challenged by Frank Slavin, Peter Jackson and Peter Maher, but nothing came of these challenges. He, however, thought there still was a good fight left in him, and challenged Jim Corbett to fight him under Marquis of Queensberry rules for $20,000 a side. Jim, to the surprise of the sporting world, and probably to that of John L., accepted the challenge.

The Olympic Club of New Orleans offered $25,000 for the fight and, in conjunction with a lightweight championship battle between Jack McAuliffe and Billy Myers and a featherweight championship battle between George Dixon and Jack Skelly, pulled off the fight on September 7, 1892, which resulted in the defeat of Sullivan in the twenty-first round.

The outcome of the contest dumbfounded the English-speaking world, as John was considered invincible, and Corbett the calf being led to slaughter. Jim's best ring work prior to that fight was a long drawn out battle with Peter Jackson and as the latter at the time was looked upon as the best heavyweight in the country the draw, practically, was a victory for Corbett. At that he was not conceded a chance against the mighty Sullivan.

It was not "who would win the fight," but, "how many rounds would Sullivan permit Corbett to stand before him." It was a case of "write your own ticket" as to the money one wished to bet on the Californian at any price, which, it was thought, was stealing money. There were a few, but only a few, that gave Corbett a chance to win, and they won handsomely on the result.

A complete story of the fight by rounds hardly is necessary, as the battle was too one-sided. Corbett, with his science and speedy footwork, went around the champion like a cooper goes around a barrel. He showed no signs of fear when he stepped to the center of the ring to shake hands and receive instructions from Referee John Duffy. He acted as if the result of the contest was a foregone conclusion, and that the $45,000 at stake was his personal property.

His defensive tactics in the early rounds, which consisted of feinting for openings and not taking advantage of those that presented themselves, and skipping all over the ring, did not meet with the approval of the Sullivanites, who hooted and jeered him and demanded he stand up and fight, as they had come to see a fight and not a foot race.

It only took Corbett two rounds to gauge the big fellow opposed to him, after which he cut loose, landing almost at will on face and body. He had John in a bad way in the fifth round and might have finished him in the next few rounds, but his seconds advised against his forcing the fighting too strongly, fearing John might score a lucky punch that would settle the fight.

Sullivan tried hard to change the tide of battle, but try as he would he could not connect effectively on his slippery and clever opponent. Although his face resembled a well-chopped hamburger steak, he was steady on his pins when he answered the bell for the twenty-first round. He still was full of fight, or, rather, he was anxious to fight, but his blows lacked steam and his judge of distance was woefully bad. His leads were easily blocked, but he was slow in raising his guard to stop the blows Jim kept shooting in on him.

Corbett stalled a bit, then suddenly tore into his tired antagonist and, before the spectators were aware of what was to transpire, he shot out lefts and rights with marvelous force and rapidity and sent the big fellow down. John struggled to his feet, but before he could regain an upright position he lunged forward, landing headfirst in the sand, and was counted out.

George Siler